Krishna's Dark Son

KRISHNA'S DARK SON

(Inspired by the Mahabharata and folk tales)

V BALAKRISHNAN

ZERO DEGREE PUBLISHING

Title: Krishna's Dark Son
Author's name: V Balakrishnan
Copyright © V Balakrishnan 2021
Published By: Zero Degree Publishing

Zero Degree Publishing
No. 55(7), R Block, 6th Avenue,
Anna Nagar West,
Chennai - 600040
Ph: 9840065000

e mail: zerodegreepublishing@gmail.com
website: www. zerodegreepublishing.com
Printed at Manipal Technologies, India.

First Edition by Zero Degree Publishing: December 2021
ISBN: 978-81-954399-0-4
ZDP Title: 43

Cover Design: Meera Sitaraman
Cover Photo: C Vishwajith
Typeset: Vidhya Velayudham
Printed at Manipal Technologies, India

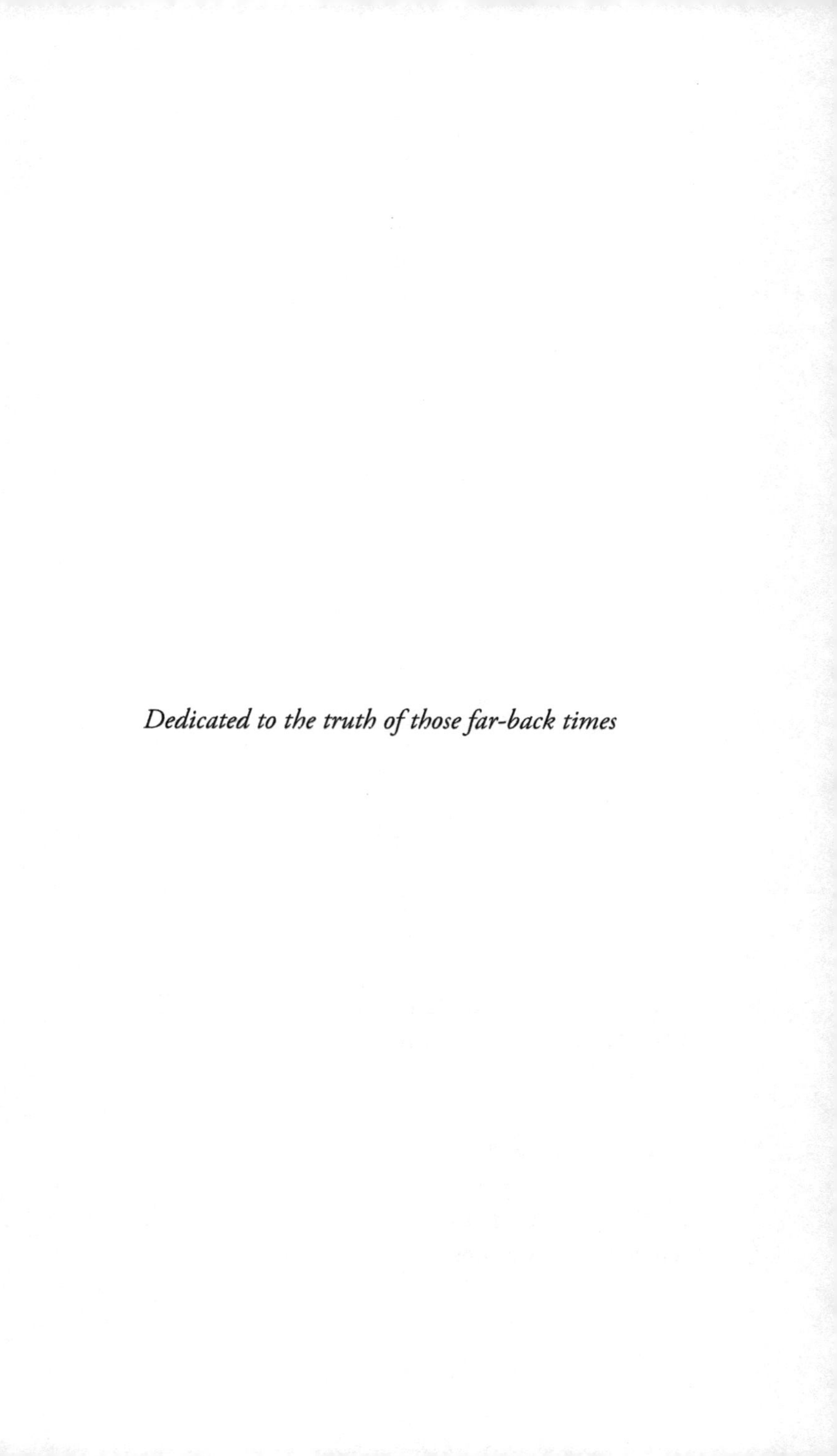

Dedicated to the truth of those far-back times

SOURCES

The Mahabharata (translations of Kisari Mohan Ganguli,
M N Dutt and Bibek Debroy)
Harivamsham
Devi Bhagavatam
Srimad Bhagavatam

The play premiered at the Alliance Française of Madras in
June 2018 and was performed by Aparna Kumar.

1

Breathe… Breathe… Breathe…
That's what we actors tell ourselves
before we delve into the mysteries of human endeavour.
I come from a long generation of storytellers.
We were your first lawmakers and educators.
Yes, laws had to be made when we transgressed.
And we transgressed when we wished to possess.
We were urged to possess for we sought immortality,
and immortality was a redundant quest,
for death does not exist in itself.
Wait, I digress, for I am a simple storyteller.
Not a living philosopher or poet.

Give me a few glasses of good wine,
and I might consider myself a brilliant actor.
And as the wine's dulcet effects reduce,
I will become an ardent critic of my own self.
I wish to continue
in the long, generous tradition of storytelling.
Generous, because of your patronage,
not my cache of stories.

That is limited and restricted,
for the laws we helped to make
have now grabbed us by the neck
and force us not to talk
or face the consequences.
But in my limited cache,
I found something inspiring today.
A story so deeply embedded
in morals, and ethics, and codes of conduct
that it became invisible to the scholars' eyes
and to the sommeliers' tastes.
Did I say "sommelier"?
Oh my god, I am so sorry!
Did I just describe a story as a wine?
To be imbibed, chewed, inhaled,
and get intoxicated with?

Wait…

That sounds fine.

A good story does have layers within it.

Casks of time, which give it a distinctive smell and body.

And I found such a story to tell you today.

But you must afford me your indulgence,

for this is a very complex story.

You must allow it to play with your palate,

and tingle your senses,

and not judge it.

And when I am done,

you can negate it.

I don't actually care.

For the secret is this:

A good fable can never be negated.

It becomes you,

creates you,

directs you,

and then… you become the story.

2

Rukmini, Satyabhama, Jambavati, Kalindi,
Nagnajiti, Mitravinda, Lakshmana, Bhadra.
Strikes a chord?
Don't worry if you can't place these names.
These are the wives of Krishna.
Him you recognize, don't you?
The Godhead, the consciousness of the universe,
the human embodiment,
who went through
Hunger, Thirst, Sleep, Fear, Lassitude,
Delusion, Sorrow, Doubt, Pleasure,
Egoism, Old age, Disease, Death,
Non-knowledge, Knowledge,

Displeasure, Envy, Jealousy,
Pride and Weariness.
Human qualities my father exhibited.

Yeah. I am his son, check the resemblance.
Come on, look at me carefully.
Do you see Krishna in me?
Maybe I am not as dusky as he is,
but see the face-cut, and my smile.
Everyone says I am Krishna's very image.
I am his own son.
My name is Samba.
Jambavati's first born.
My mother did not have any children for a long time.
She approached my father with humility,
desiring to bear him children.
So, Krishna went to the mountains
where Shiva roams with his hordes,
and there, under the guidance of a teacher,
the great Upamanyu,
Krishna grasped the staff of asceticism,
shaved his head, held a skull,
and chanted a secret incantation
that would please the wanderer of the graveyard,
and make him bestow blessings.

My father ate fruits in the first month,

nothing but water in the second.

In the third, he raised himself on his big toe,

and stood erect, head turned towards the sky,

sustaining himself on air.

Six months passed before Shiva could be compelled

to grace the Yadu.

Shiva arrived with the all-mother Parvati,

Shambhu arrived as Samba,

as *Prakriti*[1] and *Purusha*[2]:

Ardhanareeshwara[3].

The son of Devaki was overwhelmed, and fell at his feet.

He arose to address his most private needs.

Krishna spoke in a voice

that was deep as the rumbling clouds:

"Cause and creator,

I am bound by attachments

to my many wives.

I have known fear from the time

I was a foetus.

I suffered many pains in my birthplace,

---

1 Primal force of nature.

2 Cosmic being.

3 A cosmic form of Shiva, half male and half female.

I killed a woman,

I killed bovine,

I killed my own uncle.

Served as a cowherd, covered always with cow hoof dust,

and left my home again and again

in fear of enemies.

I am no king, cannot be one either.

Yayati's curse holds strong.

"Shambhu.

It's tough to be a householder.

I am dependent on everyone,

from my wives to my servants.

And my wife Jambavati feels I neglect my duties

in not being the father of her children

as I am of those of Rukmini's.

And I engaged on this ascetic path

wanting children, daughters and sons.

But now I am ashamed.

With arduous application,

your sight I obtained.

And to ask for children is demeaning to you.

You who grants freedom and liberation from eternity.

Shame on me, for being trivial and transient.

But I am bound to my wife's request

and ask you for a child.
I know I step further into the abode of sorrow.
The cause of pain.
"I go closer to destruction,
but my mind does not desist,
and demands a child as the fruition of this encounter."

Krishna fell silent,
overwhelmed with emotion.
Shambhu is a very gentle god.
He is the destroyer, but the gentlest one of them all.
He had visited my father in his ascetic role
as Samba, the man and the woman.
My father asked for a child like him.
But there is no one like him.
There is only him.
And he blessed my father
with himself,
and I was born to my mother.
And I was named Samba,
born of the grace of Shambhu.

But Parvati, the mother of the universe, spoke to my father.
When Shiva was finished, he left.
But Parvati stayed behind,

for she had some words for Krishna

that Shambhu the gentle one did not wish to prophesize.

"Your son will destroy.

Where you have descended with the objective

of destroying the race of warriors,

he will be born to destroy you and all your race.

When time shall come to pass,

the curse of the age will land on your domain.

All your sons and the others

will lose their senses from drinking liquor,

and will kill each other.

Your son, born by the grace of Shambhu,

Samba will be the cause of your end.

You prayed to the destroyer,

and a destroyer you will beget.

But grieve not.

What will be, will be.

You carry the effect of resentment,

from days of yore, of men and women whom you abhor.

And now your son you will abhor.

And he will give you cause.

But he is only the instrument of destiny's clause.

"Samba your son,

Krishna, is the manifestation of Shambhu,

but will look just like you.
Samba, born of the grace of Shambhu;
Krishna's son *Krishnamukh*[4]."
The all-mother disappeared,
and Krishna, my father,
returned to Dwaraka.

---

4 The face of Krishna.

3

I think I have been honest
in setting up the story for your pleasure.
I have allowed myself to uncork the vintage bottle,
and offer it for your olfactory palate to savour.
So now you know that Krishna had a son, Samba,
who was born to destroy the entire race of the Yadavas,
including the Vrishnis, the Andhakas, and the Bhojas.
Let me again revel in creating the illusion of the character,
and evoke Samba to take the story further.

'The great character named Samba, I evoke you.
To enter me, to take over me, and let me win.
The character of Samba, enter me.

I call upon you to become me,
as I will become you.'

When Kamsa heard Devaki's son would kill him,
he indulged in infanticide;
when Herod was told the true king of kings was born,
he too killed new-born babies.
But my father nourished me, cherished me, loved me,
and then he cursed me.
But more on that later.
Let me not get ahead of myself.
I was a happy child, spoiled rotten by my uncle, Balarama,
the great Sankarshana.

I was there accompanying my father,
when Arjuna took Draupadi for his bride.
We were told not to participate.
The Yadavas were to observe and applaud,
not enter the arena and contest.
There was some confusion regarding the rules
of who could participate, and who could not.
While the kings and their ministers
deliberated over the initial stipulations,
Arjuna had led the lady away
amidst violent protestations.

And my father as usual did not give much away,

but we were delighted to know

his cousins were alive and awake,

and we had laid to rest our bow hands,

for the Panchalas' and Pandavas' sake.

Then I too got intoxicated by my youth.

And the tales all spoke with such bravado

of Krishna snatching Rukmini

right under the nose of her betrothed and the emperor.

I too wanted to prove my worthiness

and abducted Lakshmana,

the beautiful daughter of King Duryodhana.

Abduction, a heinous crime,

that was given credibility under rules and laws.

One part of me saw all the wrong which we perpetuated

in the name of greater good and destiny;

another indulged in it with aplomb.

But this story is not validation

of an era or a character,

but the story as it was —

Iti-hasa: Thus it happened.

Not to tell you how to live,

but to let you know this is how we lived.

I abducted her from her marriage hall.

Yes, I know we were the vassals of the Kurus,

but who ponders legal ramifications

when one is in the throes of love?

Was it love? I don't know, but I was excited.

Karna, Duryodhana, and a few elders

were sent by Bhishma to capture me.

Bhishma, who kidnapped three women

from the king of Kashi

and forced them on his brother,

now launched a minor battle on me.

I stood my ground;

I was not going to look like an idiot in front of her.

I fought those splendid archers alone,

but the Kurus attacked all at once.

I was captured, trussed up, and thrown in prison.

I did wink at Lakshmana as I was being taken away

and I swear, she blushed.

Ugrasena, my great-grandfather, prepared for war,

but my uncle, Balarama, whose favourite I was

and preferred me over my brothers

—maybe because I was as fun-loving as he—

and could drink him under the table,

stopped the warriors from strapping their armours;

a war between the Kurus and the Yadus was not warranted.

He came with gifts to appease the son of Dhritarashtra

and priests to give credibility to my crime.

Duryodhana was happy to receive his guru,

and offered him fruits and water.

Balarama came straight to the point:

"Ugrasena orders you to release Samba,

whom you captured by unfair means.

He does not wish

for the unity of the family to be ruptured."

But the Kauravas were enraged.

"A shoe wants to step on a head covered with a crown.

We were decent to share our beds,

seats and meals with you;

we treated you as equals and even gave you thrones.

We looked the other way

when you paraded as royal kings

so you could enjoy the white sunshade,

and the fan of the yak tail.

But you have dared to spit

on the hand that feeds you,

and should be chastised.

We gave nectar to the snakes.

You have lost all shame.

You prospered through our grace,

and now like a sheep claiming a lion's share,

you demand—and appropriate—

that which was not granted by us,

not by Bhishma, nor Dhritarashtra, nor Dharmaraja.

None of us acquiesced or blessed your travesty."

Balarama was provoked.

He laughed and did not maintain a diplomatic posture:

"Big-mouthed, impudent, dishonest Kurus,

I believe you are not seeking peace.

We are the shoes and they, the heads?

It is stupid to seek peace,

when what they need is a beating.

Men when intoxicated by power of rule

are given to inconsistent dismal drivel.

Well, let's rid the earth of the Kauravas."

He took his plough,

and hollowed out the city of Hastinapura

and dragged her to be drowned.

Now don't ask me if a city

can be pulled by a man with a plough,

however strong he is

—even if he is Balarama—

and taken to be drowned in the river,

even if she is Ganga.

But that's how the story goes.

Maybe he threatened

to break down the dam with his plough,

and that would flood the city for sure.

Yes, that would be a worthy threat to make.

And Balarama could fight armies off by himself.

So when he said,

"Samba or drown",

it was enough to make the Kurus scramble for peace

and they got me out.

And with Lakshmana in tow,

we went where my uncle

was holding to ransom the entire city.

Uncle was easy to please with gifts and wines.

He took me away with him.

I had a bride,

and he had a good story

to tell in the court of the Yadus.

4

Well, soon it was the turn
of my elder brother Pradyumna to be besotted.
Where I had fallen for a cousin,
he fell for the enemy's daughter.
Her name was Prabhavati.
A very pretty girl,
with a very tough father.
As the case usually is.
There was no love lost for us; the Yadavas.
But, in their regions we were persona non grata.
The surest way to tempt
a hormone-ridden youth to do something
is to tell him he can't.

And we entered the kingdom of her father, Vajranabha,

the city of Supura.

And here is the fun part:

We entered as actors,

for actors were welcome in this city

because the people of the city were art lovers.

Actors are welcome in all cities.

It was a city lined with auditoriums,

amphitheatres, dance halls,

all made to perfection by the dictates of the *Natyashastra*[5].

Inside the city, as we roamed the lanes,

I wished we were not enemies.

This was not like our poets harped—

a country of brutes and beasts.

This was a kingdom with sweet people,

cultured, joyous;

they respected their women, men, and the others;

children played freely on the streets.

But my brother was in love,

and the lady too had expressed her desire to be with him.

That was ample moral grounds

to plunge two countries into war,

or two cities, or two families.

---

5 A Sanskrit treatise on the performing arts.

Why is love always dictated by binaries?

We were inside the city;

our permit passes said 'Actors'.

This was the best way to enter the city

and kidnap Prabhavati.

Maybe the word "kidnap" is not appropriate.

Prabhavati loved Pradyumna—or so he claimed.

But here we were, disguised as actors

and performing, from stage to stage,

charming the city, winning accolades.

And yes, we are quite guilty

for parents wishing to keep their young daughters

away from theatre and actors.

But don't be too hard on real actors.

We were but actors disguised as actors.

The king heard of our brilliance on stage,

and our plan was validated as we received

an invitation from the king to perform

for his palace and government officers.

The king gave us the best rooms,

and gifts beyond compare.

For those who entertain the people,

only the best will suffice.

We performed four different plays.

We played the epic poem Ramayana.

And that was greatly enjoyed.
"Hear one, hear all!
Come and enjoy, all!
The story of Sri Rama and his brothers.
This evening, at the Music Academy.
At the Museum Theatre, at Spaces, at The Backyard[6]."

(*The actor can sing and perform any classical piece from the Ramayana.*)

The citizens of that city
were astonished by our refined acting,
and threw us many gifts and jewels.
The king was enthused to invite us
to perform privately for his family, and their entourage.

We played our repertoire, sang and danced.
I was the *Vidushaka*[7] and had most fun.

(*The following is played as a comic scene, the play representation also depicts the actual occurrence of the kidnapping of Prabhavati.*)

------

6 Names of performance spaces in Chennai.
7 Jester.

King... King, come here quick!

Your daughter is in the grip of a malady.

Her door is locked, and she asks for no food.

She is definitely unwell, or in the clutches of a spirit.

Stay I will, to please the gallant king,

spy and find out what is wrong here.

But wait, is it not wrong to spy on a nubile girl?

At this age, girls like to be alone,

and fall in love with their fingers.

Admiring their beautiful shape, with nails of red.

They paint and blow upon their fingernails,

cooling the heat of the natural dyes,

and then rub away their work,

and start all over again.

Hmm, I have an idea...

I will close my eyes, and listen at the door.

That won't be a sin.

If the princess is down with a fever, for sure I will know.

There... I have reached the door of the princess' chamber.

Now I place my left ear—

the right is for listening to holy words only—

on her huge doors, and close my eyes.

Hmm, what's that sound, like her heartbeat?

It seems the princess is tapping her feet on the floor.

I believe she is struck with a terrible fever,

and in agony thrashes at the door.

Is that the sound of the poor one,

screaming through clutched teeth?

Ahha, she does not want us to know she is sick.

She wants to spare her parents the pain

of knowing their daughter is unwell.

What a blessed soul!

I will go now and report to the king,

that Prabhavati is not well and needs a doctor!

Wait, she is not alone!

I hear another voice.

Has her illness manifested itself into an *Asura*[8]?

Perhaps it is threatening her?

But she, she seems to be asking for more,

benedictions and blessings maybe.

Now the ear will not suffice, and my eye

I will have to place at this key hole.

I will bathe in the Ganga for this sin I am committing,

but the good books say

when a loved one is in trouble, to peek is not a sin.

---

8 Sons of Diti, and cousins of the gods.

Now I place my eye at the door:
Ahhhhhhhaaa… Aahhh.. Ahhhhaaaaaaaaaa
Is this a ghost or an apparition?
It's the princess
in the embrace of the actor from the other night!
And that night, we stole Prabhavati away.

5

I was considered a nuisance at Dwaraka.
I don't know why,
but I was not like the other sons of Krishna.
I was always agitated,
and my attention was all over the place.
My father sent me to learn archery from Arjuna, I learnt it.
I couldn't attach all the philosophy Uncle Arjuna spouted,
to the act of shooting an arrow.
At the end of the day, it was a bow and an arrow,
not some deep intricate mystery.
I could hit the eye of the quintessential bird, every time,
and I could see everything around the bird.
How can I negate the tree, the clouds,

and all those crowding the school of Arjuna?
Arjuna was a little disappointed in me.
He loved my cousin Satyaki,
and bestowed more time on his tutelage.
I served for some time in the court of Yudhishthira,
but got bored and returned to Dwaraka.

Around this time, a strange incident occurred
that chilled my bones.
As I was exercising on the banks of the river,
a soothsayer who made his trade by spewing pleasant lies
to self-obsessed individuals
came to me and offered to tell my future for a coin.
I was seeking amusement, and this seemed fine,
as I waited for better action to offer itself,
or for my friends to find me here.
He spread his oilskin cloth on the floor
and was running his spiel:
"Your sons will be emperors, you will conquer the world.
Your wives will be faithful to you.
You will build many temples."
I yawned. My patience was running out.
I gave him his coin.
But as his fingers touched mine,
his face changed;

his body seemed to shrivel;

his mouth was foaming;

like a mad horse, his eyes receded into his lids

till only the whites were exposed.

His fingers dug into me, in a vice-like grip.

I struggled to break free,

but he seemed to be glued to me.

He went into a trance:

"Samba, born to destroy,

stands alone with a pestle.

He pounds his family to death.

He grinds them under his feet.

Samba, you will destroy all that Krishna created.

You have within you the other half,

and when that is unleashed,

you will kill,

and you will die:

In blood

that you will cause to spill,

your destiny you will fulfil."

That was quite traumatic.

Real or a trick, I did not know.

But that roadside astrologer

had made my blood run cold.

I ran to my mother.

My mother loved me more than my father.

He had eighty children,

and to remember our names was a task.

But to my mother, I was her first-born.

I repeated what the soothsayer said.

Her face went dark.

She gained composure, and opened up to me.

She told me how I was gained by austerities.

She said I had Shiva's essence in me.

She showed me a parchment with predictions made

and recorded, as was the etiquette, when I was born.

This son of Krishna

will work to close all that is open.

He will achieve that which his father cannot.

He will repeat his father's acts and like a prodigal son,

work for the benefit of the earth.

He will be the destroyer of malignance

while he attempts to protect his allegiance;

and will create the maleficence.

The conundrum of his family's end.

I was struck with depression.

Was this to be true?

These predictions upon my predilections
made me want to end my life.

My mother, she soothed me with pleasant words.
But I was confused;
slowly driven to crazy antics,
witnessing every act of mine,
judging, probing.

Driven to anger and anxiety.
I was trying to find escape
in wine and street fights and orgies.
To leash me, make myself wake in peace,
I was desperate to be sobered by insobriety.

I was appointed a general and served the war council.
I fought alongside Balarama and Krishna
and helped win many wars.
I liked fighting and I was good at it.
I found some respite from escape in debauchery.
I was beaten badly in the war against Salva;
but Krishna and Balarama
were brilliant, and Salva was killed.
News came from Hastinapura around that time,
that the Pandavas were exiled to the forest.

Satyaki wanted me to ride in the night with him.

He said, "Let us to Hastinapura and kill

Duryodhana and his evil brothers;

and hold the kingdom for

Yudhishthira and his brothers,

until they finish their exile."

But Krishna admonished him,

and told us not to interfere

in the Kuru clan's matters.

Krishna was the commander-in-chief

as far as King Ugrasena was concerned,

and his word was law.

Even Balarama was not happy

with what Krishna was doing,

and where it was all going to lead.

He too wanted to punish the Kurus,

and bring the Pandavas back from the woods.

But Krishna refused the thought,

and said dharma wouldn't be served.

Dharma[9]: a double-edged sword;

but I did not care.

─────────────

9 An individual's duty fulfilled by observance of custom or law.

If Krishna said
"Go and fight the Kurus",
I would have.
He said don't; I did not.

"Go and fight the Kurus",

6

One day when I was resting,
news came from Pradyumna
that Narada was in Dwaraka,
and Krishna wanted us to attend to him.
I was not in the mood to listen
to his sweet talk and boring stories,
and did not go.

He was a wandering minstrel,
erudite and a wonderful storyteller.
But he had a penchant for causing trouble
just to prove he could.
I heard later Narada was organizing

a get-together with special wines
and he wanted me to come.
This seemed more up my alley.
As I entered the boisterous room,
thick intoxicating fumes—incense, laughter—
men and women laughing in corners: a regular party.

Suddenly, Krishna called out in a loud voice:
"Samba!"
I was scared. Why was Krishna so angry with me?
I found out later that Narada had been up to no good;
he had told Krishna
that I was having affairs with his concubines,
gawking at their naked bodies,
and bathing with them when it pleased me.
And that one of his junior wives Nandini
had actually been in bed with me.
Narada had made sure
all the concubines were in a drunken stupor,
and when Krishna asked them for the truth,
they in their senseless intoxication giggled
and showed passion for me.

Narada went on to say
I was taking advantage of looking like Krishna,

and seducing his wives.

Krishna was not happy with me.

He started scolding me.

I listened, protesting, for a long time.

But then I lost it.

Even a father has no right

to scold his son without reason in public,

to make him seem like a criminal.

Krishna could have chastised me in private.

I replied; I shouted, spewed rage;

maybe I misbehaved.

I don't remember things I said in anger.

But Krishna concluded with:

"You have behaved with arrogance;

you are a disgrace to our family.

I cannot tolerate you anymore;

the sight of you is repulsive to me."

And when I replied in rage,

without a moment of hesitation—

in front of my mother—

he cursed me with leprosy.

My body grew sores.

Pus and blood oozed from them.

Everyone avoided me,

even my wives and children.

But my mother,

she did not lose hope,

and got me one cure after another.

Twelve years it took for me to heal.

I was told I needed to bathe

in the river to be cleansed

and thank the gods.

I was so weak I could not even rise;

my father carried me to the river to bathe.

He bathed me like a new-born.

Finally, he forgave me

for what I had never done.

Later, as I gained strength,

I visited places where the Sun God was worshipped.

When a person is down with things they cannot explain,

much succour is revealed

in matters of esoteric substance.

I was praying hard to the Sun God to cure me,

for only the rich rays of the morning sun

were helping my affliction.

I built two temples to enhance his worship.

Sometimes the irony of the situation made me smile:

We were *Chandravamshis*[10] seeking refuge in the sun.

―――――――――

10 Those who belong to the lunar dynasty.

By the time I was fully cured,

a lot had passed.

The sons of Bharata met at Kurukshetra

to decide who would reign at Hastinapura.

Eighteen days of mindless slaughter.

Kurujangala was wrecked by a family feud.

The Narayani army, which was under my command,

was completely decimated.

Offered to Duryodhana as the Yadavas' share.

At Kurukshetra, it was Arjuna, my teacher,

who shred them to pieces of flesh,

while they stood brave

with those who took the oath of destruction, the Trigartas.

And eighteen days stood their ground, those gopalas,

until every one of them was slain.

None of us participated in the great war;

Krishna forbade us.

Only the Narayani went with Duryodhana,

led by Kritavarma;

and Satyaki and my father stood by the Pandavas.

A bloody massacre.

Everyone dead.

And my father—blamed for the carnage,

for not allowing peace to reign—
Krishna returned to Dwaraka.
He was not the god-like man who had departed;
he seemed squeezed thin, lacking life and lustre.
He was no longer the man people sought refuge in,
prayed to, and loved.
He seemed tired, tired all the time.
He did not allow anyone to see that he was
disturbed and broken behind his perpetual smile.
But I am Krishnamukh.
And I knew something was terribly wrong.
I knew my father's mind, and its workings,
as if it were my own.
And I knew, if Krishna did not have responsibilities
to shoulder, work to be rendered,
he would have been a Samba.

Later, Satyaki told me over a cup of wine
that Queen Gandhari had lost her composure
and lashed out at Krishna:
"Your family, your entire clan,
like mad dogs will tear and kill each other.
You will yourself kill them all, and die like prey
at the hands of a common hunter."
Krishna believed the words of the pious queen;

he believed in her, the worshipper of Shiva,
and knew that the words of Gandhari only reiterated
what Parvati had warned him of
when I was promised by Shambhu.

But then, if the destruction of the world
was what was sought,
then why not lead the Yadavas into the Kurukshetra war?
Why divide the massacre into two halves?
What mystery was there to suffer in knowledge
that the inevitable will come to pass?
Gandhari's curse foretold another massacre,
convulsions to tear us all apart.

I was confused. I liked things straight and clear.
Not these esoteric riddles for me.
Satyaki said everything is ordained,
and he gave me a wry glance:
"Samba, son of Krishna,
born of the grace of Shambhu,
maybe you know more than you let on."
I was not amused, and let Satyaki go.

The words of the soothsayer
who had blabbered on the sea shore

and Gandhari's curse… did they have some connection?
Did Gandhari mean for Krishna to kill his own
as she blamed him for killing her family?
Or did the curse propagate me
to be the initiator of a dastardly act?
Krishna or Krishnamukh?
But my fate was only just unfurling
and what was to lead to the second biggest massacre
inside thirty six years in Bharata,
was not my anger or skills as a warrior,
but my usual disdain for holy men
who go around pretending to be know-it-alls
and my skills of make-up and acting.

My old bête noir Narada,
with Vishwamitra and Kanwa, came to Dwaraka.
Wandering minstrels and mendicants
who had deep secrets hidden in their troves,
respected by all the elders.
The boys wanted to have some fun,
and they asked me to dress as a woman.
Before I could gauge what we were doing,
the lure of dressing imprisoned me.
They hid a mace under my garments.
We went to the holy men,

and I pretended to be Vabhru's wife.
The boys asked the old men
to determine the to-be-born's sex;
the wise old men saw through my disguise,
felt insulted and screamed:
"This heir of Vasudeva
named Samba
will give birth to an iron bolt;
and that will cause the annihilation
of all your tribe!
You wicked boys, drunk with pride,
you will see it now cause the extermination
of all you love.
Krishna will die… So will Balarama."

The curse was uttered with such conviction
that Krishna called for a council
and advised that we must be prepared:
"What will be, will be,
but action on our part must not lax.
We must maintain stoic vigil on our paths and deeds."
In a few days, I experienced great pain.
And as the Rishis had prophesied,
an iron bolt was ejected from my body.

We were all scared.
Ugrasena ordered that the iron bolt
be ground to fine powder
and thrown into the sea.
Manufacturing wine and intoxicants was banned,
and death by impalement was announced
for anyone who broke the law.

Fishermen reported to me
that when the powder was thrown into the sea,
the tides reversed and threw it back on the beach.
When I went to the shores,
I saw the black powder everywhere.
In a week, green erka grass grew where the particles
had embedded themselves.
Every time I passed that place,
I felt a melancholic doom invade my soul.
Nothing was right in the city.

7

Death was wandering inside our houses,
while we struggled to avoid an inevitability.
Death roamed about in the form of a man,
terrible and scary, bald, black, and tawny.
He was seen by the Vrishnis,
as he peered into their houses;
the archers tried to shoot him down,
with hundreds and thousands of arrows.
But how to pierce the destroyer of all creatures?
How to kill the deathless one?

The winds blew stronger,
the stench of putrefying flesh rent the air.

The omens were all awful and forebode destruction.

Rats and mice swarmed the streets,

eating the hair and nails of sleeping women.

Earthen pots cracked and broke

without any cause apparent.

Birds of prey entered our homes

and chirped and chirped without pause, night or day.

Goats imitated the hooting of jackals.

Parrots hooted like owls.

Many birds appeared impelled by death,

pale in complexion, in various hues of red.

Pigeons flaunted in the houses of the Vrishnis,

an angry disposition not generic to them.

Asses were born to cows,

mouses to the mongoose.

There was no shame among the citizens

as they committed acts of sin.

They insulted the elders, the teachers, and the departed.

They stopped the worship of gods.

Wives deceived their husbands.

Husbands deceived their wives.

Fires when ignited blew their flames

to the inauspicious left;

sometimes it burned with

the splendour of blue and red.

The sun seemed in a perpetual eclipse,

when rising or setting over the city,

surrounded by headless trunks of human forms.

Food in the kitchen, well-boiled and clean,

was seen covered by worms of various kinds.

When the priests were receiving gifts

from well-meaning people

or when the high-souled engaged in silent recitation,

the heavy tread of innumerable men could be heard; yet

no one was seen to whom the footsteps could be assigned.

The constellations were being attacked by planets.

No known constellations were seen.

None one was born under could be sighted.

When Krishna blew the *Panchajanya*[11] to ward off evil,

it was greeted with the dissonance

of asses braying in awful voices.

Krishna noticed it first.

The day of the new moon coincided

with the thirteenth and fourteenth lunations.

Krishna knew what it meant.

He was there when it had happened before.

It was the time of the great battle of the sons of Bharata

when Rahu impinged on the fourteenth lunation

____

11 Krishna's conch shell.

to render it to the fifteenth,

and when it appeared again,

signalling the perverse course of time,

Krishna knew another destruction was to follow.

It was thirty six years to the day

since Gandhari had cursed us.

Burning in grief at the death of a hundred sons,

deprived of all her family,

she had decided what was to transpire.

And now the omens reiterated her words with evil pride.

Krishna addressed us all together:

"The present is exactly similar to that time

when the son of Dharma noted these awful omens

even as the two armies arrayed themselves to die.

We need to purify ourselves and pray.

So, I propose we make a pilgrimage

to the sea coast at Prabhasa,

to bathe in the sacred waters and redeem our sins."

I went cold.

Prabhasa.

Is that not where the erka grass grew?

The manifestations of the iron bolt

that ripped me open

and announced the death of my clansmen.

I stared at Krishna.

Krishna took me by the shoulder,

and we moved to a corner.

He spoke:

"Gandhari's words have to come true.

Samba, born of the grace of Shambhu,

Krishnamukh, you know this better than I do.

Where we were born to detoxify the earth,

we, the purifiers, have become the toxins ourselves.

Now, Samba, you have to

redeem your work on earth

and destroy us.

It was not by chance that you dressed as a woman

when you challenged the Rishis with your mischief.

I saw Shiva as Shambhu when he granted me you.

Now, Samba, assist me

in this final deed we have to perform.

Get ready, my son, for one more theatrical venture.

Organize the Vrishnis to make this journey

to the sea coast, to bathe in the holy waters."

I went about this work.

Organized messengers to reach out to all,

helped set up food and wine and fresh fruit.

Suddenly the food was cooked before time,

the fruits ripe and sweet

in vulgar abundance.

The worms were missing.

All seemed to be urging us to get ready for the trip.

The final trip.

The destination of death awaited us in glory.

How it was to be, I don't know,

but I was excited that death beckoned us.

8

Around this time,
the Vrishni ladies dreamt every night
that a woman of dark complexion and white teeth
entered their homes,
laughing and running through Dwaraka,
snatching away their sacred wrist threads.

The men dreamt that a terrible vulture
entered their homes and fire chambers,
and gorged on their bodies.

Terrible apparitions snatched away their flags and armour.
Krishna's chakra, the Sudarshana, sank into the earth.

Agni's gift to him when he burned the Khandava

descended into the mud

unable to bear the blood it had shed,

unable to rest in the hands of the one it had been gifted.

The chariot of Krishna

was yanked away by the horses he favoured.

Daruka, the charioteer, was unable to stop the steeds

from dragging the chariot into the ocean.

Warriors dreamt of beautiful women urging them

to start on the pilgrimage,

where they would be met by *apsaras*[12]

and could rejoice in pleasure.

The flag of Krishna went missing, stolen maybe.

And when it was found in a thicket,

the Garuda was missing from it.

I decided to surge for the pilgrimage.

The omens were pressing upon us.

I was curious to see what the curse

of those wandering men would offer.

And as a blazing retinue we set out,

on horses and elephants.

I was in charge of setting up tents and organizing food,

---

12 Female celestial singers and dancers.

and I made sure abundant was available.
Krishna was bidding goodbye
to the wise men and the teachers,
many deciding to depart from the world
by yogic manipulations.
Krishna did not stop them.
He had no disposition to prevent them.
We reached Prabhasa and pitched camp.
The warriors behaved rudely,
taking food that was set aside for the priests,
soaking it in wine and throwing it to the monkeys.

The sons of the house of Vrishni began their revelry;
barrels of wine, blares of trumpets,
burlesques of actors and dancers.
Balarama, my uncle, loved his wine.
And he began to drink and roared for more.

Kritavarma, the survivor of the Kaurava army,
Satyaki, the warrior who wanted
to defeat Duryodhana single-handedly,
Krishna's younger brother Gada,
Pradyumna, Vabhru, Aniruddha,
everyone began to drink.
I could see the events unfold.

I could see what the culmination was going to be.
Like a bad play whose climax is known in the first act,
I could see how this was going to end.

It started with Satyaki, drunk with wine,
He laughed at Kritavarma in the midst of the revelry
"What warrior would with weapons kill sleeping men?
You, Kritavarma, are an animal!
You supported Ashwatthama in killing soldiers in sleep,
and we the Yadavas will always hate you for it."

Pradyumna applauded Satyaki for this abuse.
Kritavarma made a rude gesture at Satyaki
and emphasizing his disregard for him, spat out the words:
"You call yourself a warrior…
When you killed
an unarmed man on the battlefield.
Bhurishravas was in yogic meditation
when you cut his head off."

Krishna was incensed upon hearing these words
and glared at Kritavarma.
Then Satyaki goaded Krishna, saying,
"Kritavarma was involved in the murder of Satrajit,
Satyabhama's father."

Old skeletons were tumbling out,
tempers rising and sides forming.
Satyaki rose, screaming, drunk, roused:
"Kritavarma... you killed my best friend Drishtadyumna
and the sons of Draupadi, and the sinless Shikhandi.
Now you will pay for that sin."

Fables from thirty six years ago, suddenly became
the truth of the moment.
Satyaki leapt up and cut off Kritavarma's head.
He did not stop there, attacking everyone.

Krishna ran to prevent him, but Kritavarma's relatives,
impelled by the perverse hour,
surrounded Satyaki and attacked him.

Krishna stopped in his tracks,
for the character of the hour was revealed.
The sight of the heroes rushing to attack a drunk Satyaki
caused no anger in him; he stood unmoved.

Pradyuma, enraged, jumped to Satyaki's aid.
Not everyone had weapons, but used the pots and pans
from which they had been eating.
Pradyuma and Satyaki fought like fiends,

but were slain even as we watched.
Time became the master of ceremonies.
As all began to strike each other,
destiny made them clutch the erka grass,
which turned into deadly weapons in their hands.
Krishna plucked the grass and hurled it
at all who came to assault him.
The others followed his actions,
and each blade of grass was now a thunderbolt.

The curse of the wandering mendicants was coming true.
He who hurled a blade of grass
saw it pierce through everything.
Even the utterly impenetrable.
Inebriated with wine, they fell on each other
and burned in destruction.

I was the initiator of the carnage
worse than Kurukshetra, where
at least once in a while dharma reigned.
Here it was a bestial feast.

I plucked a blade of grass
and it in my hands became a trident.
I jumped into the melee

and I do not know whom I killed.

I spared no one, not

my brothers, my sons, nor my grandsons.

Krishna was slaughtering with no compunction.

Perfection born from destruction.

All had to die for the earth to survive

and future generations to come.

I was struck by many weapons.

I dropped on the field.

As I was about to die, I saw Krishna leave.

Everywhere there were corpses.

I raised my eyes to the sky.

Vishvedeva had come to escort me to the otherworld.

Samba, born of the grace of Shambhu,

Son of Krishna, Krishnamukh,

the actor who initiated death,

made his final exit.

9

They say when such a character is created,
the actor must allow the spirit to enter her
and then allow the spirit to leave her.

(*The actor performs a made-up ritual to exit the character.*)

And this must be done with a meditative quality,
so no vestige sticks to one's true self.
For I don't want to go back home,
projecting the son of Krishna on my family members.

People ask on many occasions,
"Is this story true?"

But what is the truth?

And what is a lie?

It is what we believe.

That which enhances us is the truth.

What does not, becomes a lie.

The Mahabharata as we know it today,

was compiled from over fifteen hundred sources.

But I confess, this character has become a friend.

Empowers me, makes me see the world

through his sad eyes,

makes me question

the double-edged sword of dharma.

I love to share the story of Samba,

born of the grace of Shambhu,

Krishna's son Krishnamukh.

May truth prevail, happiness reign.

THE END

Acknowledgements

My salutations to the writers, story-tellers and playwrights whose works have inspired me all my life to explore the squillion aspects of *The Mahabharata* again and again. I would like to express my gratitude to the prodigious translations of the epic by Kisari Mohan Ganguli, M N Dutt and Bibek Debroy.

V Balakrishnan is an actor, playwright, designer and an ICCR empaneled director. An alumnus of the Shri Ram Centre for Performing Arts and the National School of Drama, New Delhi, he is a Charles Wallace Scholar and a recipient of the Fulbright Distinguished Award in Teaching. Balakrishnan is the founder and artistic director of Theatre Nisha, Chennai, and has over 200 productions to his credit. His play *Sordid* won The Hindu Playwright Award 2019.